The Protoctist Kingdom

The Protoctist Kingdom

MARC ZABLUDOFF

Marshall Cavendish
Benchmark
New York

Marshall Cavendish Benchmark
99 White Plains Road
Tarrytown, New York 10591-9001
www.marshallcavendish.us

Library of Congress Cataloging-in-Publication Data
Zabludoff, Marc.
The protoctist kingdom / by Marc Zabludoff.
p. cm. — (Family trees)
Includes bibliographical references and index.
ISBN 0-7614-1818-0
1. Protista—Juvenile literature. I. Title. II. Series.

QR74.5.Z33 2005
579—dc22
2004021821

Front cover: Trypanosomes with red blood cells
Title page: A diatom
Back cover: Trychonympha protoctists in a termite's gut
Photo research by Linda Sykes Picture Research
The photographs in this book are used by permission and through the courtesy of: Eye of Science/Photo
Researchers, Inc.: front cover, 71; Jim Zuckerman/Corbis: 3, 54; Alfred Pasieka/Science Photo Library/Photo
Researchers, Inc.: 6, 55; Jeremy Burgess/ Photo Researchers: 8; Mehau Kulyk/Photo Researchers, Inc.: 13;
Corbis Royalty Free: 16 (left). 16 (middle). 17 (right), Clouds Hill Imaging Ltd./Corbis: 16 (right); U. S.
Fish and Wildlife service/George Gentry: 17 (left); M. I. Walker/Photo Researchers, Inc.: 18; Wim van
Egmond/Visuals Unlimited: 20; Sinclair Stammers/Photo Researchers, Inc.: 22, 52, 67; George Musil/Visuals
Unlimited: 23; Dr. David Phillips/Visuals Unlimited: 26; John Pacy/Photo Researchers. Inc.: 28; Laguna
Design/Photo Researchers, Inc.: 29 (left); Eric Grave/Photo Researchers, Inc.: 29 (right), 43, 50; Michael
Abbey/Visuals Unlimited: 31, 32, 46, back cover; K. W. Jeon/Visuals Unlimited: 35 (top left), 35 (top right);
Photo by David Porter, University of Georgia: 36; David Scharf/Science Photo Library/Photo Researchers,
Inc.: 38; Darlyne A. Murawski/Peter Arnold: 39; Bob Evans/Peter Arnold: 40; David W. Gotshall/Visuals
Unlimited: 44; Thomas D. Mangelsen/Peter Arnold: 45; Peter Arnold: 47; Steve Gschmeissner/Photo
Researchers, Inc.: 48; SPL/Photo Researchers: 58; Richard Kirby, David Spears Ltd./Photo Researchers, Inc.:
61; Dr. Dennis Kunkel/Visuals Unlimited: 62; Bill Bachman/Photo Researchers, Inc.: 64; Manfred Kage/Peter
Arnold: 69; Andrew Syred/Photo Researchers, Inc.: 73. 74; Dr. Gene Feldman, NASA GSFC/Photo
Researchers, Inc.: 78; Alexis Rosenfeld/ SPL/Photo Researchers, Inc.: 79; Roland Birke/Peter Arnold: 80;
Carolina Biological Supply/ Visuals Unlimited: 86 (top left); Jerome Paulin/Visuals Unlimited: 86 (bottom
left); A. B. Dowsett/Photo Researchers, Inc.: 86 (top right); Andrew J. Martinez/Photo Researchers, Inc.: 86
(bottom right).

Printed in Malaysia

Book design by Patrice Sheridan

1 3 5 6 4 2

CONTENTS

Single-celled, ocean-dwelling radiolarians exist in a great variety of forms, yet they make up only one small part of the vast kingdom of protoctists.

Worlds of Wonder

Sometime in 1674, in the thriving Dutch city of Delft, a self-taught scientist named Anton van Leeuwenhoek looked through a hand-made microscope at a drop of local pond water. Shimmering in that drop, two hundred times larger than life, he spied impossibly tiny creatures swimming about.

"Very little living animalcules, very prettily moving," Leeuwenhoek later wrote in amazement. The little "animalcules" were single-celled organisms and not really animals at all, though Leeuwenhoek could not have known that. He did know, thanks to his microscope, that he was probably the first to see them since the day they were created. Most likely he would have pegged the date of their creation at some few thousand years before his own. He would have been off, though—by a billion and half years, more or less.

Microscopes were a fairly new invention in seventeenth-century Holland, and Leeuwenhoek's were among the first and the finest. A merchant, Leeuwenhoek had begun making magnifying lenses to examine closely the cloth he bought and sold. But he soon turned his eye away from fabrics and toward the world at large—or the world at small, to be precise.

Leeuwenhoek was astonished by the universe revealed through his lenses. He was so entranced that he spent fifty years peering through his microscopes at every object he could think of. He looked at the stingers of bees and the hairs on fleas, at water from ponds and water from puddles, at scrapings from teeth and tongues, at skin and blood and urine and other bodily substances. Each look was a visit to a new world of wonders. In scum floating on a pond he found "some green streaks, spirally wound serpent-wise." Each hair-thin strand he saw was composed of "very small green globules joined together." In puddles he found his animalcules "very gently moving, with outstretched bodies and straightened-out tails."

Leeuwenhoek wrote of his discoveries to scientists around the world. He gave them detailed instructions on how to build microscopes such as his, and he urged them to look at the tiny beings for themselves. They did, and over generations they began to compile a long list of the "microbes" they found. The animalcules they called protozoa (from the Greek words meaning "first animals"). The green globules they decided were plants, and they lumped them together under the name algae.

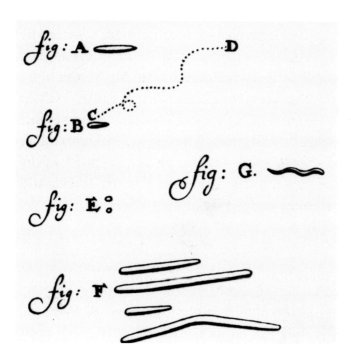

Three centuries ago, Anton van Leeuwenhoek accurately drew the "animalcules" he saw through his microscope; today we know them as bacteria (shown here) and protists.

LEAVES OR LEGS?

Plants and animals—what else could anyone have called the things? For centuries educated people had known that all Earthly life came in only those two forms. The principle had been stated clearly two thousand years earlier by the Greek philosopher Aristotle, and in all the years since no one had any cause to question it.

Aristotle was surely not the first person to try and make some sense of the world. The need to impose order on what appears to be chaos is a natural human desire—ask any parent confronted with the horror of a child's messy bedroom. All of us arrange our homes and our possessions in a way that makes sense to us, if for no other reason than to make things easier to find.

But Aristotle was the first to establish categories for the living things he saw. And he made two main categories: plant and animal. Within the animal category he placed more than 500 different creatures, bundling them together in what he thought were appropriate groups. He based these groups on the animals' appearance, or their behavior, or on the way they produced babies. Thus, he put all birds in one group, all animals with tusks in another. He was observant enough to realize that dolphins, which breathe air and nurse their young, should be grouped with animals like dogs and goats rather than with the fish the dolphins outwardly resemble.

After Aristotle, the notion that humans could discover the order of the natural world was taken for granted. But exactly what that order was, and how it came to be, was often a matter of dispute.

SCIENCE STEPS IN

The modern system of classification really did not get its start until the end of the seventeenth century, when an Englishman named John Ray (1627-1705) compiled two enormous catalogs of plants and animals. These catalogs arranged thousands of different living things into groups based on details of their appearance. For animals, the details were mainly found in teeth and toes, which turned out to differ noticeably from one group to another.

Ray's work was greatly enlarged by the Swedish scientist Karl von Linné (1707-1778), who is most often known by the Latin version of his name: Linnaeus. Linnaeus was the one who laid the foundation for the way we classify all life-forms today. He also set the rules by which we assign names to different types, or species, of living things.

Linnaeus devised a system of "binomial nomenclature," in which we assign two names to every living thing on Earth. The first name is the name of the genus, the large group of related animals or plants to which the organism belongs. The second name is the name of the particular species. All names, Linnaeus declared, should be in Latin so that scholars all over the world would be able to communicate in one common language.

To use a familiar example: House cats and cougars are alike enough to belong to the same genus, and so both have the same first name: *Felis.* But they are clearly not quite the same animal. So house cats are further identified by the species name *catus,* while cougars are identified by the species name *concolor.* (By tradition, genus names are capitalized, while species names are lowercased; both are written in italics.) The two are shown by their names to be similar, but different. For humans, *Felis catus* makes a warm companion; for *Felis concolor,* it makes a warm lunch. The system applies also to plants and animals that are no longer with us.

Linnaeus and scientists who came after him added other, higher categories to the system, groups broader than genus and species. All genera (plural of *genus*) were gathered into families. Families were then grouped into orders, orders into classes, classes into phyla (plural of *phylum*), and phyla, finally, into kingdoms. Each higher category had broader qualifications for membership and so, more and more members. Each one of these categories is called a taxon (plural, taxa), and so the science of classifying living things is called taxonomy.

To continue the cat example: the genus *Felis* is part of the family Felidae, which embraces cats of all kinds, from lions to lynxes, and tigers to extinct sabertooths. All those cats are then held within the order Carnivora, which joins lions, tigers, and not just bears, but sea lions too. Their class, Mammalia, puts them in the warm-blooded company of whales and weasels and all other mammals. Their phylum, Chordata, puts them together with all animals that have a spinal chord—even lumpy sea squirts. And their kingdom, Animalia, combines them together with all other animals, period, alongside every slinky lowlife that ever existed.

Taxonomic Tips

The proper order for the main taxonomic levels used today is
- Kingdom
- Phylum (for animals) or Division (for plants and fungi)
- Class
- Order
- Family
- Genus
- Species

Generations of students have devised clever aids for remembering these taxa. One old favorite is the phrase **K**ing **P**hilip **C**ame **O**ver **F**rom **G**ermany **S**tewed. Another is **K**eep **P**lates **C**lean **O**r **F**amily **G**ets **S**ick.

THREE KINGDOMS?

Linnaeus went far in cleaning up the messy variety of life he observed. But he did not question the basic assumption that two, and only two, kingdoms of life existed. The first challenge to that notion came from the German biologist Ernst Haeckel (1834-1919) in 1866.

Haeckel was a firm believer in the theory of evolution proposed by Charles Darwin in 1859. Darwin said that the similarities we see between species reveal a common history. Dogs, wolves, and jackals—or chimps, gorillas, and humans—did not all suddenly appear simultaneously, with all their striking similarities. They came from a long line of shared ancestors. Over great periods of time some of those ancestors changed, or evolved, and the family tree split into branches. Animals that are very similar, like dogs and wolves, split apart relatively recently. Animals that are very different, like horses and horse flies, must have split apart much, much further back in time. All of them had to have evolved from much simpler creatures that lived many millions of years earlier.

Haeckel realized that the tiny organisms Leeuwenhoek first saw might well be those earlier creatures. In their simplicity and small size, they were very different from all other living things. In fact, they were so different that they could be the ancestors of plants and animals both. But if they were ancestors to both, then obviously they could belong to neither one kingdom nor the other. They belonged in a kingdom of their own. Haeckel called his new realm of microscopic beings the Kingdom Protista and its members, protists.

Haeckel's addition of a third kingdom of life suggested a huge change in the way scientists could think of, and use, the science of taxonomy. A century earlier, Linnaeus had grouped together species whose appearance or behavior were similar: lions with tigers, pine trees with fir trees. But he made no assumptions about how such species were related to one another. In his time, scientists generally believed that all species on Earth were created by God at the same time, just several thousand years earlier. By carefully noting the similarities and differences between species, they believed, they could better understand God's plan.

According to Darwin's theory of evolution, however, when we gather species into groups, we are doing more than mapping similarities. We are also revealing the history of life, showing how one form gave birth to another, over millions of years of evolution. Haeckel was absolutely certain that Darwin was right. And he was equally certain that his protists revealed what the first kingdom of life looked like.

For decades, most biologists dealt with the issue by ignoring it. Two kingdoms worked well enough most of the time. Besides, the idea of something being alive that was neither a plant nor an animal just did not seem to make any sense. Who needed such problems?

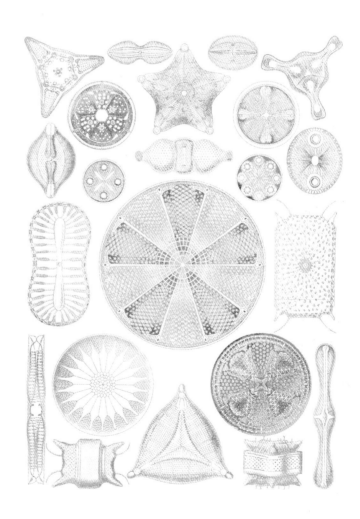

German biologist Ernst Haeckel produced exquisite illustrations of the protists he studied, including these diatoms, with their intricate, glasslike shells. (This illustration has been colorized by a computer to show details.)

But by the mid-1950s, scientists could no longer put the issue aside. They had learned too much about how different single-celled organisms were from everything else. Even worse, they had realized that within the world of single-celled organisms there were two main groups, and that the differences between them were enormous—even bigger, in some ways, than the differences between the "microbes" and all other plants and animals.

Over the years, increasingly powerful microscopes had shown that one group of organisms—the bacteria—were all rather simple compared with the other. The chief difference was that bacteria had no nucleus—a dark circular unit within the cell that contains the cell's genes, its chemical instruction manual. All other single-celled organisms did have a nucleus; some even had many nuclei. It seemed that these more complicated cells had to have evolved from the simpler bacteria. And the appearance of a nucleus seemed to be a major event in evolutionary history.

FOUR KINGDOMS? FIVE?

In 1956 American biologist Herbert Copeland (1902-1968) suggested that Haeckel's three kingdoms should really be four: one for plants, one for animals, one for bacteria alone, and one for all the other protists, the ones with nuclei. Three years later, biologist Roger Whittaker (1924-1980) took Copeland's scheme one step further and proposed a system of five kingdoms. The new one was for fungi, such as mushrooms and molds. Whittaker's research showed that fungi were remarkably different from the plants with which they had always been grouped.

Whittaker's five kingdoms were Monera (the kingdom of bacteria, from a Greek word meaning "single"), Protista, Fungi, Animalia, and Plantae. Today, most—though certainly not all—-scientists accept this basic five-part division of life, although with some ongoing disagreements.

For instance, biologist Lynn Margulis, who is one of the world's leading authorities on the subject, prefers to use the name Protoctista (which means "first created") rather than Protista, and to call the organisms within the realm protoctists (rhymes with "provoked this") rather than protists. Her reason is that scientists have traditionally used *protist* to refer to single-celled creatures, but the kingdom actually contains some large, multicelled organisms also. To avoid confusion, she says, better to use a new name.

A Word on Words

In practice, scientists throughout the world use both protist and protoctist. For the sake of clarity, however, this text uses the kingdom name Protoctista, and refers to collections of individuals as protoctists. To make reading a little easier, though, *protist* is used whenever possible, to refer to the smaller inhabitants of the kingdom.

It is unfortunate that so many of those tiny inhabitants have large and difficult names—names like *Pelomyxa pelustris* or *Euglena gracilis*. But it is not surprising. We have common, everyday names for the animals and plants we have long been accustomed to seeing—like *robin* or *snake*—but not for those things that were never part of our lives, for example, *Pterodactyl*. If the ancient Romans or Greeks had possessed microscopes, maybe we would have common names for thousands of protists.

Of course, if the Romans or Greeks had known about dinosaurs, maybe we would have sensible names for all those creatures too—like Godzilla, instead of *Tyrannosaurus*. But we have adjusted to the demands of those extinct giants. Maybe we can adjust to the demands of the little guys too.

THE FIVE

Many scientists divide Earth's

ANIMALIA

polar bear

FUNGI

mushroom

MONERA

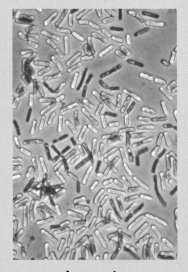

bacteria

KINGDOMS

life-forms into five kingdoms.

PLANTAE

pitcher plants

PROTOCTISTA

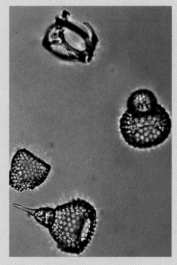

radiolarians

17

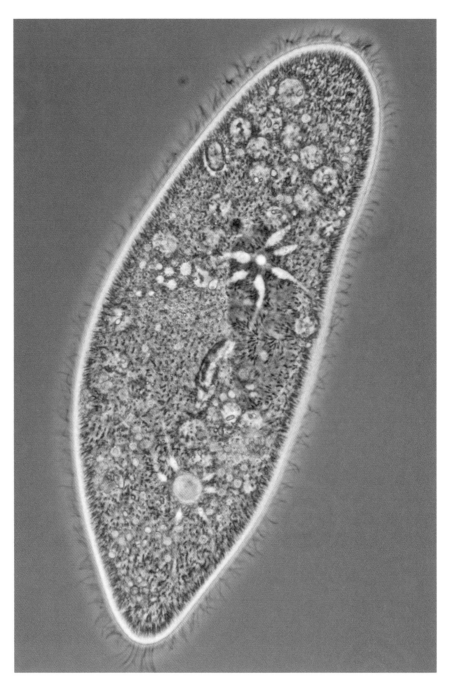

A paramecium is a typically tiny protist, no more than a few thousandths of an inch long, but it is a fully functioning, independent organism.

A Small Problem of Identity

So who exactly are these small beings with large names? That's not so easy a question to answer. The protoctists are a *very* large and *very* varied group, with perhaps 250,000 species. But there could be as many as 600,000. No one yet knows for sure.

For convenience, scientists determine membership in the protoctist kingdom by what an organism is *not,* rather than by what it *is.* If an organism is not an animal, plant, fungus, or bacterium, it is a protoctist. This strategy works well in separating these ancient organisms from the others whose basic design evolved later. But it results in a large kingdom, in which some members seem to have nothing in common with others.

One thing most protoctists do have in common is that they are usually invisible. A few protoctists can grow quite large—the giant kelp, for instance, a kind of seaweed, can stretch more than a hundred feet (30 meters). Other protoctists, such as green algae found on the surface of ponds, gather in large, easily seen colonies. But huge numbers of protoctist species are made up of single-celled organisms that are visible only through a microscope.

A cell is the basic unit of living things. Even the smallest commonly seen plants and animals are made up of millions of cells. And a large animal—a typical human, for example—has about 100 trillion (100,000,000,000,000) cells, each with its specialized task. We have blood cells, skin cells, liver cells, kidney cells, nerve cells, muscle cells, and so on. But many organisms on Earth—most organisms, actually—are complete beings made up of only a single cell. The smallest of these are bacteria, which are typically only a few micrometers, or millionths of a meter, from end to end. Some are smaller than half a micrometer—smaller, that is, than .0005 millimeter, or .00002 inch. Next up in size are the single-celled protists, which are generally ten times the size of bacteria. Even a 100-micrometer beast of a protist, though, is a tiny tenth of a millimeter long (.004 inch).

But small does not mean simple. The tiniest protist is still a fully functioning organism. It breathes, it produces energy, it moves through the

Some members of the family of chalk-shelled protists called forams, like the one on this matchstick, are single-celled giants, large enough to be seen with the naked eye.

world, interacts with other life-forms, reproduces, and dies. And it does all these things in interesting and unfamiliar ways. Furthermore, just because most protoctists are small does not mean that they are hard to find. In fact, precisely the opposite is true. Protoctists are everywhere—they are in the seas, in lakes and ponds, in rivers and streams and swamps and mudflats, on the ocean floor and the forest floor, and, believe it or not, in us. They live within the watery tissues of our bodies, happily carrying on their lives without our ever being aware of them—unless, of course, they cause some sort of disease.

A handful of protoctists do make us sick. A few can actually kill us. But they do not pick on humans exclusively. Protoctists live in or on nearly every plant, animal, and fungus on Earth, on every continent, and in every sea. In some ways, protoctists have been far more successful in colonizing the planet than sophisticated humans have been. Humans, after all, occupy only a small fraction of the surface of Earth, and none of the land or water below. But then, we have been on Earth for only a few million years. Protoctists have been around much, much longer.

THE PROTOCTIST SAGA

Protoctists can boast of an ancient pedigree. The first of their kind evolved sometime between one and a half billion—1.5 *thousand million*—and two billion years ago. Yet protoctists were actually latecomers. By the time they arrived, life's party on Earth had been bubbling along for some two billion years already. These earlier residents were the bacteria, and they are the protoctists' direct ancestors.

In its earliest days, Earth was not an easy place to live. It was very hot, for one thing. And it had little oxygen. Today, the oxygen in our atmosphere is produced mostly by plants and algae, which manufacture it from the carbon dioxide gas they take in. Where did the oxygen come from before there were any plants to produce it? From bacteria that were able to

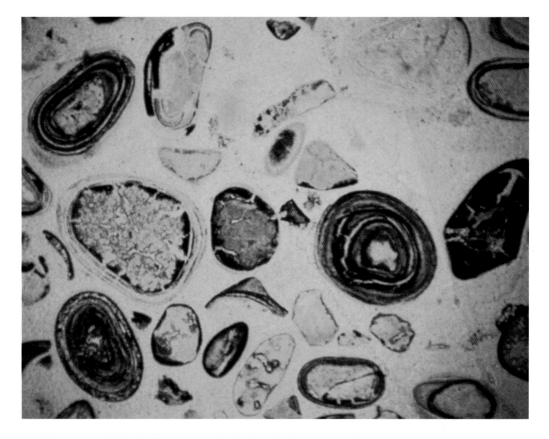

Two-billion-year-old fossils show pieces of cells that look very much like modern algae, suggesting that the first protoctists appeared an extremely long time ago.

"breathe" the sulfur- and hydrogen- rich air of early Earth. Oxygen was poisonous to these early bacteria, as carbon dioxide is to us humans today. So the bacteria got rid of the oxygen.

With each infinitesimally small breath, these pioneering bacteria exhaled a tiny bubble of oxygen. Breath after breath—by billions upon billions of bacteria, over thousands of millions of years—eventually filled Earth's atmosphere with oxygen. Gradually, bacteria evolved that were able to make use of the once-poisonous gas. And gradually these bacteria prepared the Earth for a different kind of cell.

ANATOMY OF A CELL

To a biologist, the difference between a bacterium and a protist is far greater than the difference between a *T. rex* and an earthworm. Through a microscope, even an untrained observer can immediately see the distinctions.

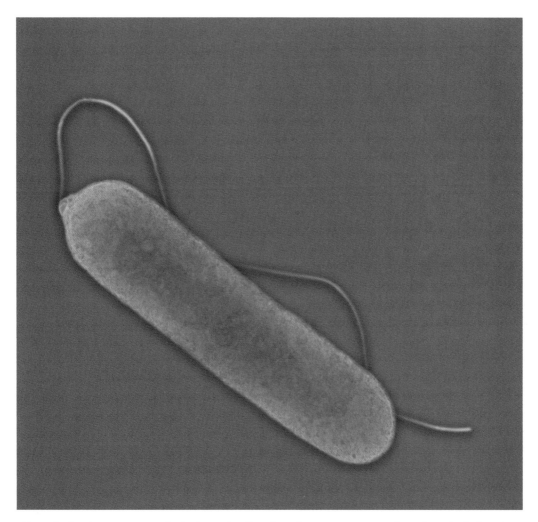

Magnified, a bacterium reveals the long, thin flagellum that it uses to move through its thick, liquid world.

Compared with all other life-forms, bacteria are simple things. They look more or less like transparent cylinders. The cells have a fluid interior, called the cytoplasm, that is held together by a stiffer cell wall. The cell wall is lined with a thin, more flexible "skin," or cell membrane. There are no smaller structures within the cell, no specialized parts or compartments. The genes of a bacterium—the bits of the chemical called DNA that tell the cell what to do—are all contained on a single circular strand that floats within the cytoplasm. Outside the cell wall is a kind of tail called a flagellum (plural, flagella). Bacteria move by rotating their flagella in a corkscrew motion.

A protist, in contrast, is not only much larger, it is much fuller. The protist is not a bland blob like a bacterium. It contains a lot of very distinct smaller structures within it, and they make this cell a vastly more complex and highly organized organism.

The most important of these structures is the nucleus. Indeed, it is the lack of a nucleus that separates the bacteria from all other forms of life. Cells with a nucleus are called eukaryotes ("you-CARRY-oats"), a name that comes from the Greek words meaning "true kernel" or "seed." All animal, plant, fungus, and protoctist cells are eukaryotes. Cells without a nucleus—bacteria—are called prokaryotes (the prefix pro- means "before," indicating that these cells evolved first). The nucleus is separated from the rest of the cell by its own thin membrane. Inside the nucleus the cell's genes are strung like beads on a number of thin strands called chromosomes.

Outside the nucleus, there are many other distinct parts within the cytoplasm. Precisely what kind of parts, and how many, depend on the particular cell we're looking at. But the most important are the mitochondria and the plastids. These are specialized units that produce energy—the mitochondria by "breathing" oxygen, the plastids by making use of sunlight. All animal cells depend on mitochondria. All plant cells rely primarily on plastids. Protoctists may make use of either, or both.

Any one of these smaller units within the cell is called an organelle. Eukaryotic cells, whether they're single-celled protists or members of a human body, have lots of organelles. Prokaryotic cells—bacteria—have none.

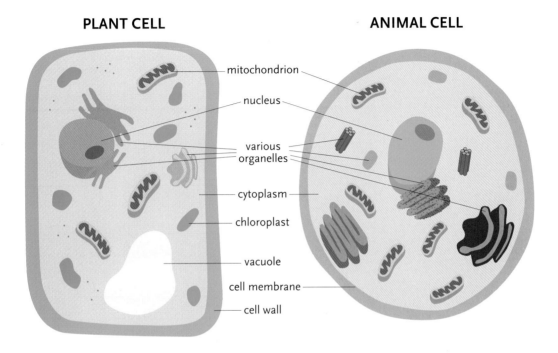

PLANT CELL

ANIMAL CELL

mitochondrion

nucleus

various
organelles

cytoplasm

chloroplast

vacuole

cell membrane

cell wall

Though plant and animal cells are very different, they share some of the same types of cell structures. Some protoctists have features similar to animal cells, some resemble plant cells, and others look a little like both.

BUSIER CELLS

Protoctist cells, then—for convenience, let's think of them as individual protists—are bigger and fuller than bacteria. But they have another obvious difference. Protists are also more lively than bacteria. It is not just that protists move around more. Many do, in fact, but some hardly move at all. Rather, it is that the liquid interior of the cell—the cytoplasm—is in constant motion. It streams throughout the cell, moving along a network of fine tubes that stretch across the cell like an interstate highway system. These tiny tubes, known as microtubules, were an important innovation in life's evolution, and all life-forms that have evolved from protoctists—meaning, all life besides bacteria—

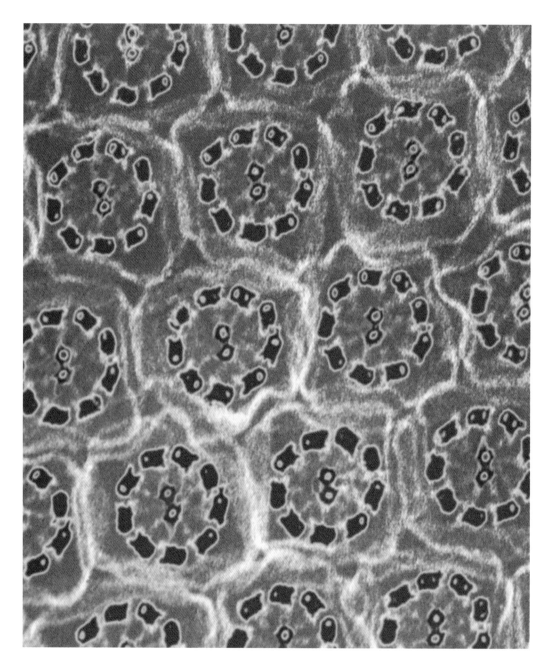

Each strand in a protist's whipping tail is made up of twenty tiny tubes arranged in a "telephone dial" pattern—two tubes in the middle surrounded by a ring of nine pairs of tubes.

have kept them. Microtubules are found in every cell of every plant, animal, and fungus that has ever existed, and they have many uses. In our nerve cells, for instance, they provide the "wires" along which messages travel.

In many protists, these tiny tubes provide the cell with not just an internal transportation system but also an external one. It turns out that twenty microtubules, bundled together, form the structure of the whipping tails that propel protists through their watery world.

These "cell whips" look similar to the flagella of bacteria. Many scientists, in fact, refer to them as flagella. However, the eukaryotic tails are quite different. First of all, they are made of microtubules bundled together, like strands of wire in a cable. Bacterial flagella are not. And these eukaryotic microtubules are arranged in a very specific way. One pair of microtubules is surrounded by an array of nine more pairs, in what has been called a "telephone dial" pattern. Finally, these tails do not rotate as flagella do. Rather, they whip back and forth.

To distinguish these whipping protist tails from the corkscrewing flagella of bacteria, some biologists use the term undulopodia, from a combination of ancient Greek and Latin words meaning "waving feet." Undulopodia are more powerful motors than flagella, and better able to move the bigger cells.

REPRODUCTION

Since most protoctists are simply single cells, one would think the business of making more protoctists would be rather straightforward—as with bacteria, for example. Bacterial reproduction seems easy. Bacteria moms make bacteria babies without the need of bacteria dads. Actually, the words "mom" and "dad" are meaningless for bacteria. Each bacterium reproduces by splitting in half. Before the split the genes are copied, and a new set goes to the new cell. Thus the new "baby" cell is an exact copy of the parent cell.

Bacteria reproduce asexually—they split in half, and each "daughter" cell is a copy of its "mother."

Animals and plants do things differently. They have sex cells—sperm and eggs—that must combine before a new individual can grow. Each sperm cell or egg cell has just half the normal number of chromosomes—the strands on which the genes are gathered. Not until the sperm and egg come together does the cell have the full number of chromosomes it needs. The interesting thing about this method is that when egg and sperm fuse, the genes they carry become mixed. The result is that the new cell is a combination of genes from both "mother" and "father."

Protists don't embrace either the bacterial method or the animal and plant method. They use both. And they use them in a confusing manner. Some types of protists always reproduce sexually, like plants and animals. Others always reproduce "asexually," like bacteria. Still others, like insects, go through extraordinarily complex life cycles that have many distinct stages—sometimes dozens of stages, with the protist changing form in each one. In some of these stages the cells simply divide. In other stages they must combine with other cells before reproducing. Sometimes, one of these stages is a "resting" state. When conditions are not ideal, the protist surrounds itself in a hard shell, called a cyst, and essentially shuts down. When things get better, the cyst wakes up and forms a new organism.

Complicating things still further is that in the single-celled world, sex and reproduction do not always go together. *Reproduction,* for a protist, means the creation of a new organism. *Sex,* for a protist, means the exchange of genes. Some protists have sex without reproduction, some have reproduction without sex, some have both but not at the same time. Many protists need to exchange genes regularly with other protists. If they don't, they die. But these exchanges do not always result in new cells.

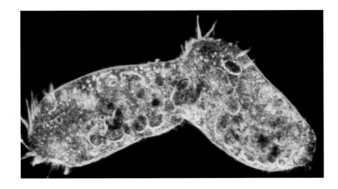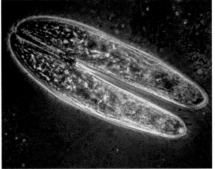

Protists, like bacteria, may simply divide to produce offspring (left), but they may also first join together to exchange genes (right).

Getting Along for Evolution's Sake

All the specialized bits and pieces that power eukaryotic cells today—the photosynthesizing chloroplasts, the oxygen-using mitochondria, the whipping cell tails—make them very different and more complex than their simple bacteria ancestors. But if these complex cells evolved from the simple cells, where did all this high-tech machinery come from?

From the bacteria themselves, according to protoctist pioneer Lynn Margulis. She is a champion of the theory that evolution sometimes proceeds through symbiosis, by two organisms coming to live together as one. Chloroplasts, for example, are plastids filled with the green-colored substance called chlorophyll. Most plants use chlorophyll to turn sunlight into energy. Margulis, however, notes that chloroplasts have a striking resemblance to certain free-living bacteria that also contain chlorophyll and depend on the sun for their survival. Algae—and ultimately, plants—got their start, she says, when bacteria like these were "eaten" but not digested by an early eukaryotic cell. The captured bacteria eventually came to live as part of the larger cell and became necessary for its survival.

Margulis believes that there were a number of important symbiotic events like this in eukaryotic history. Mitochondria too were probably once tasty but indigestible bacteria, she says. Among the evidence, she notes, is that even today, after more than a billion years of shared history, mitochondria and chloroplasts still remain somewhat independent of the cells in which they live. For instance, they divide independently, reproducing on their own schedule and not the cell's.

Most scientists today accept Margulis's theory about the origins of these cell structures. But what about the remarkable undulopodia, those whipping improvements on a bacteria's corkscrewing flagella?

Just like other parts of the eukaryotic cell, undulopodia, she believes, were once free bacteria that somehow took up residence in a protist. Not all scientists agree with her on this point. But an intriguing example of symbiosis is given by the protists called mixotrichs, which live inside the gut of termites. Without these protists, the termites could not digest the wood they eat. And without some helpful bacteria, the mixotrichs could not move around. Instead of undulopodia, the protists use hundreds of wriggling bacteria called spirochetes that attach themselves all over the surface of the protists. The bacteria twirl their motors, the protists move to the food, the wood is digested, the termite and its tenants get the energy they need, and everybody is happy.

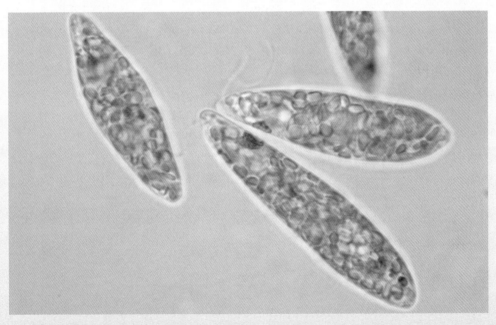

Like plant cells, many protists, such as this *Euglena gracilis* are packed with green organelles called chloroplasts, which allow them to turn sunlight into energy.

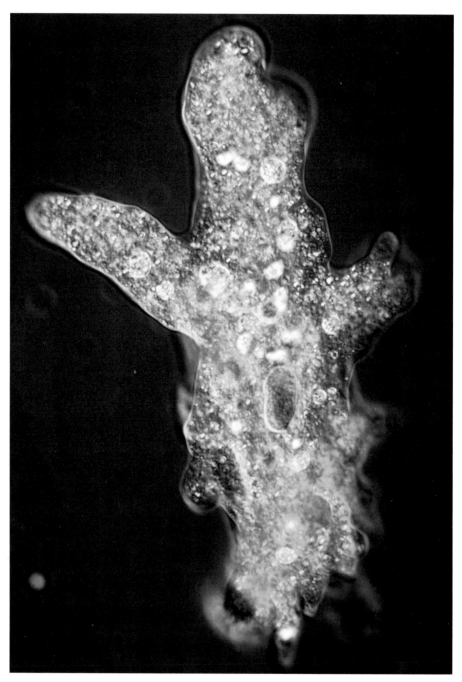

Amoebas are disconcerting because they are constantly changing their shape—an odd characteristic for a living thing.

Creeps and Slime

AMOEBAS

Among the few protoctists that are somewhat familiar to most people are the creepy-crawly amoebas. The amoebas are a large group—about 200 species, not all of whom are very closely related. What they all have in common is their lack of definite shape (*amoeba* comes from a Greek word meaning "change,") and their oozing mode of movement.

Amoebas are constantly changing the way they look. They are cells whose flexible cell wall is constantly pushed and poked by the streaming cytoplasm within. Pushing out on the skin of its cell, the amoeba forms pseudopods ("false feet") that grab onto the surface and pull the amoeba along.

Amoebas live in a wide variety of watery habitats. Some live in swamps, some in lakes, some in the intestines of animals. One species, *Entamoeba histolytica,* frequently finds a temporary home in human intestines, where it can cause serious pain and diarrhea.

Most amoeba species belong to the phylum Rhizopoda, and are rather small. Some are as tiny as one micrometer (.001 mm, or .00004 inch). But one amoeba species, *Pelomyxa pelustris,* is a mammoth among microbes. The "giant amoeba" can be a monstrous 5 millimeters long (or across—amoebas do not really have any ends to them). Granted, in our human-scale world it is only a dot, at best, but it is an easily visible dot, and that alone makes it remarkable.

More remarkable, though, is its antiquity. The giant amoeba is one of the most primitive of the protoctists, a member of the phylum Archaeprotista (*archae* means "ancient"). Like all protoctists, it has a nucleus. Indeed, it has hundreds of them. But it has no chromosomes in its nucleus. Nor does it have any energy-producing mitochondria, or any of the other organelles commonly found in more complex protists.

What it does have however, are some permanent bacteria tenants. Living inside *P. pelustris* are three different kinds of bacteria that apparently generate energy for the amoeba, as mitochondria do in other species. They also may help to get rid of "waste" substances that could poison the cell.

How did the bacteria get inside the amoeba? Sometime in the distant past, these bacteria were probably "eaten" by an amoeba ancestor but not digested. Somehow they lived on inside the larger creature. They stayed and made themselves useful in exchange for free food. Now after many millions of years of evolution, the amoeba has grown quite dependent on its guests for its own continued existence. Experiments have shown that if the resident bacteria die, the amoeba dies also.

The giant amoeba, like its distant primitive ancestors, does not like a world rich in oxygen. Too much oxygen, in fact, will kill it. It lives only in the muddy bottom of freshwater ponds, where it dines on smaller protists—mostly algae—and bacteria. Its method of hunting is slow but effective. Once it senses that food is nearby (it can detect the presence of certain telltale chemicals), it starts creeping toward its prey on its pseudopods. Changing shape continuously, the mighty creeper gradually works its way up to its hapless victim. Then the amoeba completely surrounds the prey with pseudopods. Once it is engulfed, the touching pseudopods fuse, and the food is sealed within a small chamber called a

 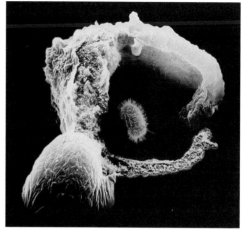

When an amoeba senses food, such as a smaller protist, it pushes out pseudopods, or "false feet." They surround the prey, then fuse together, and the food is engulfed.

vacuole. Like a bubble in a lava lamp, the vacuole passes from one end of the amoeba to the other, while the food inside is digested.

An amoeba's slow, creepy way of getting around is rather alien to energetic, directed creatures like ourselves. Perhaps that's why the amoeba has inspired so many grade-B horror movies. One Hollywood-styled amoeba, in the 1960 movie, *The Angry Red Planet,* was supposedly a Martian killer that stretched the length of a full football field. As if the oxygen-wary, bacteria-dependent, 5-millimeter-long *P. pelustris* were not strange enough!

SLIME NETS

Even the amoebas are not the kings of protoctist weirdness. They are easily beat by the slender, peapod shaped creatures known as the labyrinthulids, which belong to the phylum Labyrinthulata (from the Latin for "little labyrinth," or "maze"). More conversationally, they are known as the slime nets.

Just as their name implies, slime nets live and work in a world of slime,

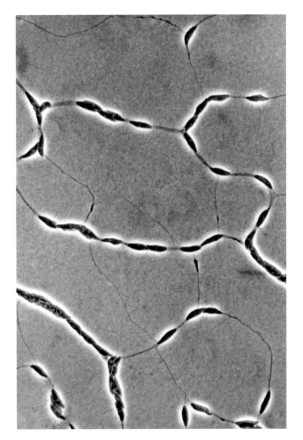

Slime nets are protists that live as communities completely within a maze of slimy trails that they produce. Outside the slime, the protists cannot move.

which they secrete, or release, from special tiny structures near the cell membrane. They do not live individually. Slime nets live as a large community of cooperating single cells that together create an elaborate network of slime "trails," along which they move.

These trails—which are actually more like tunnels to the tiny creatures themselves— are absolutely essential for the slime nets. Scientists do not know exactly how the slime nets propel themselves along the trails. But they do know that if the slime nets are not completely covered with slime, they cannot move at all. Without the slime, these protoctists are like cars with no roads to run on. With the slime trails, though, the slime nets become like cars racing down a Los Angeles freeway. Of course, they are only "racing" from their point of view—the slime nets only reach a top speed of a few hundredths of an inch per hour.

Scientists also know that the slime trails themselves move, and that the slime nets within actively search for food. When the slime nets sense that food is nearby, they secrete substances that break down the cell walls of their prey. The slime nets then absorb the contents.

Most slime nets are sea dwellers. They are commonly found living on grass growing on the bottom of shallow bays. One type particularly likes to establish its slimy colonies on eel grass, which is an important plant in areas favored by clams and oysters. Sometimes the slime nets grow so abundantly on the eel grass that the habitat is destroyed, and the clams and oysters are killed.

If anyone is casting for a horror movie, slime nets are definitely worth a look. Even if most members of the colony are killed at the end of the movie, there is still hope for a new colony—and a sequel. Any surviving individual slime nets will gather together and form a hard clump, or cyst. The cyst will just wait patiently until conditions are again right. Then they will arise, open up, and release new slime net cells to build a new slimy community.

SLIME MOLDS

If slime nets are still not creepy enough, there are always the slime molds. Despite the similar names, slime molds and slime nets are not closely related—they belong to different phyla—although they do show an obvious fondness for oozing. Slime molds are truly bizarre life-forms that utterly confuse the boundaries between kingdoms. At various times, biologists have classified them as plants, as animals, and as fungi. Some still do. But most agree that they belong properly with the protoctists.

Slime molds start out as individual amoebas crawling through damp soil and decaying leaves on a forest floor. So long as there are sufficient bacteria for them to eat in their tiny territory, they continue as lone hunters and feeders. But as they continue to reproduce, dividing themselves in half again and again and again, their food supply gets used up. When it is gone, the amoebas begin "talking." They release a chemical that signals all the slime mold amoebas in the vicinity to gather in one spot.

Precisely what happens next varies from one species to another, but the life cycle of the slime mold *Dictyostelium* offers a good example. As the call

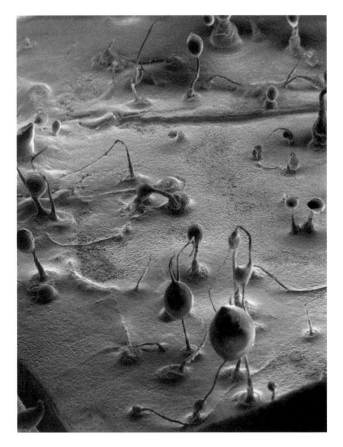

These microscopic stalks of *Dictyostelium* slime mold each began as a collection of independent amoebas that have merged to become a single large cell with many nuclei.

goes out, *Dictyostelium* amoebas start congregating, crawling over and on top of each other to form a mound. The mound grows taller and taller until finally, it just falls over. From this point on, the cells begin acting as one unified organism rather than a crowd of individuals.

The mound covers itself in a coat of slime and stretches out into something resembling a slug. This newly formed sluglike mass oozes itself over the ground toward a nice sunlit spot. There it stops and begins yet another, even more amazing transformation. It grows upward in a long thin stalk, on top of which perches a rounded bulb. Inside the bulb are many spores, tiny hardened cells that are protected against heat and dryness. When a breeze blows by, the spores are released and carried to new territories throughout the forest. Eventually, when the spores become moist, they will become new amoebas creeping off in search of food, and the cycle will begin again.

Slime mold congregations vary greatly in size from about 1 millimeter to 100 millimeters (roughly 4 inches). And they come in many shapes and colors, from round berries to delicate puffballs, from pink, yellow, and white, to red, orange, and purple. Many biologists are extremely fond of these complicated organisms. Some collect slime mold species the way other people collect baseball cards.

The aptly named pretzel slime mold (*Hemitrichia serpula*) forms a spreading mass of linked tubes; when the outer walls break down, threads with attached spores emerge.

Kelp, a form of brown algae that grows in underwater forests, is by far the largest member of the protoctist kingdom, reaching lengths of 100 feet or more.

Algae: The Unplants

Most people are at least familiar with the word *algae*. They associate it with some scummy, vaguely vegetable-like growth seen on the surface of ponds and lakes and by the seashore. So it is hardly surprising that nearly everybody thinks that algae are part of the plant kingdom. Until rather recently, most scientists also thought of algae as plants. Even today, many books continue to refer to them as plants.

But in truth algae are as far removed from plants as we humans are. They are actually members of the Protoctista. They were some of the first members, in fact, appearing on the scene at least 1.5 billion years ago.

It is easy to understand the misunderstanding. First of all, many types of algae are green. Like plants, they get the energy they need to live through the process of photosynthesis—they use the sun's light to make food from water and carbon dioxide. In the process they give off oxygen. Second of all, many forms of algae, especially the kind we call seaweed, look like plants. They seem to have stems and leaves, and are more or less rooted to one spot. As is usual in the strange kingdom of Protoctista, though, appearances are deceptive.

All photosynthesizing protoctists are algae, and there are many thousands of species, spread across hundreds of genera, and grouped into at least half a dozen phyla. (To appreciate how great a range that is, remember that we humans share the single phylum Chordata with creatures as different as birds, fish, and frogs.) The most convenient way of grouping this enormous cast of characters is by color: there are the green algae (phyla Chlorophyta and Gamophyta), the yellow-green algae (Xanthophyta), the red algae (Rhodophyta), and the brown algae (Phaeophyta).

EASY BEING GREEN

Green algae are among the most noticeable protoctists. We often call them by the inelegant though descriptive name "pond scum." Various members of the more than 16,000 species of green algae inhabit virtually every waterway on the planet. And somewhere among them almost surely is a species that represents the ancestor of all plants alive on Earth today.

Like plants, green algae are green because they carry within them the green pigment chlorophyll. This is the chemical substance that enables plants and algae to convert sunlight into usable energy. The chlorophyll is neatly contained in specialized units within the cell called chloroplasts. (*Chloro* means "green," and chloroplasts are green plastids. Other protists carry slightly differently colored, and differently named, plastids.)

Green algae take on many different forms. Some are single cells floating on the surface of the water. Many others live in vast communities of cells. Some, like *Acetabularia*, look like centimeter-wide pinwheels. Others, like *Spirogyra*, form beautiful, delicate filaments that join together in the scummy growth of a pond. And some, like *Caulerpa*, take on the strange, near-plant-like appearance of seaweed. *Caulerpa* is one of the protoctists that people often notice, since it can grow several feet long and is readily seen washed up on beaches. Few people realize how strange this common beach litter is, though. Despite its size and looks, *Caulerpa* is not a collection

Green algae belonging to the genus *Spirogyra* grow in long, threadlike colonies. Inside the individual cells, green chloroplasts are wound in delicate spirals.

of millions of specialized cells, as any proper plant would be. Its cells do not have true cell walls separating them from one another. In some ways, a three-foot-long *Caulerpa* is just a giant single cell with millions of nuclei and chloroplasts within it. Bizarre for a plant; typical for a protoctist, though.

THE RED AND THE BROWN

Although more dissimilar in color, red and brown algae actually come closer to looking like true plants than green and yellow-green algae. Like plants, red seaweeds are made up of many specialized cells. They live along the shore and far down in the sea—as deep as 585 feet (180 meters) below the surface. There they attach themselves to rocks. Unlike their green distant cousins, red algae use the reddish portion of the spectrum

Red algae, which produce their energy from the red portion of natural sunlight, are a source of food for many animals—and people.

rather than the green. (Red algae carry out photosynthesis in units called rhodoplasts rather than chloroplasts—*rhodo* means "red.") Green light is not useful to an organism on the seafloor because green light cannot penetrate through the hundreds of feet of water above. The red light that filters down toward the seaweeds is dim, but apparently it is enough. Some species of red algae grow several feet long, with branches and "leaves" that wave gently in the ocean currents.

These algae may not be real plants, but that minor distinction does not keep people from treating them like plants. Red algae are frequently harvested for food in many parts of the world. In Japan they are used in sushi. In New England, species of red seaweed are dried and sold as "dulse." (The labels on packages of dulse often refer to their contents as a "sea vegetable"—perhaps because "weed" or "algae" does not sound as appealing. But really, dulse is no more a vegetable of the sea than a tuna is a chicken of the sea.)

Red algae are an important food source for oysters and clams as well as people. They are also tremendously important in biological and pharmaceutical laboratories around the world. They are used to make agar, the substance on which colonies of bacteria are grown for medicines and research. More important to children no doubt is that red algae are also commonly used in thickening ice cream and other foods.

Brown algae grow even larger than red ones—much larger. These seaweeds are the largest protoctists in existence, with some stretching out hundreds of feet. Generally, brown seaweeds are ocean dwellers. Many types grow along rocky coastlines on both the Atlantic and Pacific sides of the United States.

One very familiar example is the giant kelp that grows in huge "forests" along the California coast. California sea otters are especially fond of these forests: the kelp is a favorite food of sea urchins, and sea urchins are a favorite food of the otters. Otters also use the long strands of the kelp as a kind of anchor. At night they wrap themselves up in the kelp leaves to keep from drifting away from their pack while they sleep.

Sea otters like kelp because the giant protoctists serve as food for sea urchins, the otters' favorite prey. The kelp are also handy nighttime anchors for sleeping otters.

Other types of brown seaweed live far from land. *Sargassum,* for example, is a seaweed that grows in huge numbers in a part of the Atlantic that has come to be known as the Sargasso Sea. There it covers an enormous shifting area of about 2 million square miles of ocean and creates a habitat for animals found nowhere else on Earth.

YELLOW-GREEN

Often joining the green algae in their scummy habitat are yellow-green algae. There are some 6,000 species of yellow-greens, contained within the phylum Xanthophyta (*xantho* is Greek for "yellow" and *phyta* means "plant"). Like the greens, the yellow-greens exist as both single cells and as colonial groups.

What sets them apart are the yellowish pigments they carry in organelles called xanthoplasts. Also, they behave in a manner most unusual for a "plant"—they move around under their own power. They swim by means of two tails at one end of the cell that whip back and forth rapidly to propel the algae through the water.

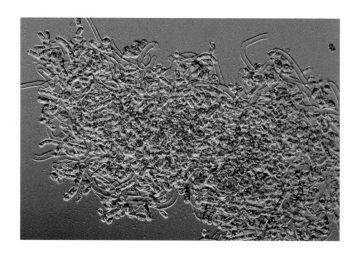

Yellow-green algae are protists that usually live together in large, branching colonies, but they can also live as single cells, moving through the water with their whip-like tails.

EUGLENIDS

Related to the yellow-greens are another yellowish group of algae that have an even more unplantlike feature: they not only move, they also "see" where they are going. These algae usually have only one tail, but they make up for the shortage with a structure that appears as a dark spot in the cell. This "eyespot" is apparently sensitive to light. Although biologists are not certain, it is possible that the eyespot is connected to the tail. It may help direct the swimming protist toward sunlight.

Eyespots are also found in a group of protists, called the euglenids, that show how difficult it is to divide the living world into just plants and animals. Indeed, it was a one-eyed, one-tailed, swimming, photosynthesizing euglenid that annoyed Ernst Haeckel so much that he created a separate kingdom for it.

Scientists have identified some 800 different species of euglenids, in both freshwater and saltwater. Euglenids have chloroplasts, like plants, and get their energy from sunlight. But they also swim and crawl like animals. More confusingly, some species, like *Euglena gracilis,* can hunt down and eat tiny particles of food. Exactly how *Euglena* behaves depends on the conditions in which it finds itself. In the dark it hunts like an animal. In the light it photosynthesizes like a plant.

So which is it—a bizarre hunting plant or a photosynthesizing animal? As Haeckel decided, it is neither. It is just a normal protist.

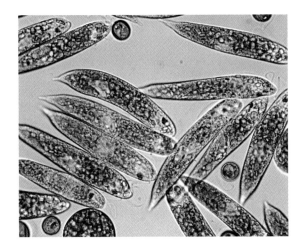

On *Euglena gracilis* a kingdom was built: its ability to both photosynthesize and hunt convinced scientists that it was neither plant nor animal but something else entirely.

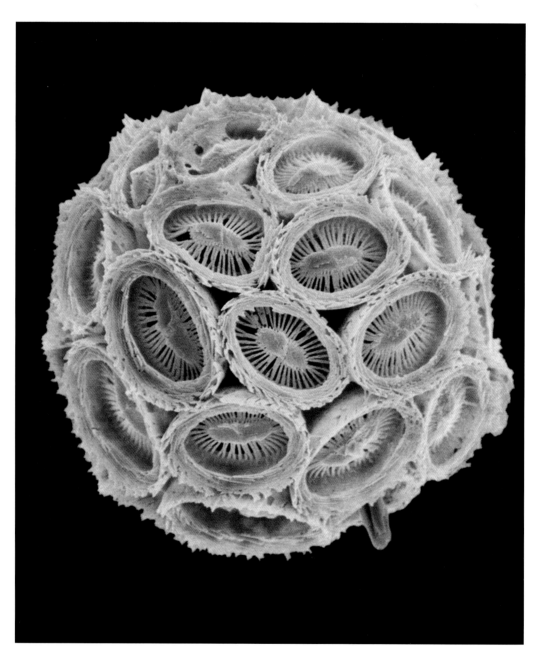

Ocean-dwelling coccolithophorids surround themselves with beautiful shells made of chalk plates. When the cells die, the plates separate and sink to the seafloor.

The Sculptors

Human children are routinely told to drink their milk so that they will have strong bones and teeth. The important ingredient in the milk, of course, is the element calcium, and humans are not alone in needing it.

Calcium is a crucial chemical for all cells. Without the proper amount of calcium cells are unable to reproduce or move. But too much calcium can destroy a cell, so it is very important that a cell gets rid of any calcium it does not need. Over millions of years of evolution, many animals have found ways to make use of the extra calcium they secrete by turning it into protective armor. Calcium combines with other chemicals to make not only bones in us but shells for snails and clams—and shells for protists, too. In this regard, protists are no different from oysters, except that protists are much more inventive when it comes to design.

COCCOLITHS AND FORAMS

Among the most beautiful creations in all of nature are the tiny shells called coccoliths, which comes from Greek words meaning "berry" and "stone." They are also among the smallest, so small that it takes many "stones," overlapping, to cover a single-celled protist in a protective sphere. Coccoliths come in many shapes. Among them are delicate spoked wheels, pointed snowflakes, and circles of joined pentagons.

Technically, the protists that create these shells are called coccolithophorids ("berry-stone bearers"), but more casually they are known as chalk-makers, which is fortunate since it is so much easier to say.

Chalk is actually a very pure, very white form of limestone, which is made of calcium carbonate—the same stuff that forms coccoliths and the shells of shellfish. The huge chalk beds we see today around the world—in southern England, northern Denmark, Kansas, along the Gulf Coast—were all formed at the same time in Earth's history, more than 65 million years

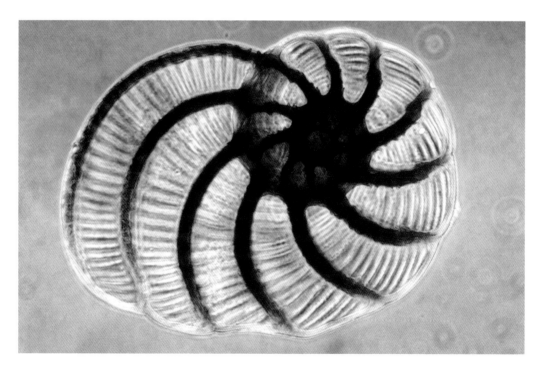

The shells of forams are also made of chalk. Over millions of years, shells from countless protists formed England's White Cliffs of Dover and other huge chalk beds.

ago. They were laid down along the bottom of the shallow seas that covered much of Earth's surface during the Cretaceous Period, when dinosaurs roamed the land. So distinctive are these deposits that they gave their name to the period—*Cretaceous* comes from the Latin *creta,* meaning "chalk."

Obviously, the seas in which the Cretaceous chalk and limestone formed were filled with huge amounts of calcium carbonate. But where did it come from in the first place? From the shells of protists—billions upon billions upon billions of them. Among them were not just uncountable hordes of berry-stone bearers but also other shell-making protists called foraminifera, or forams, for short. Foram species come in all sizes, from tiny 10 micrometers (.00039 inch) ones to "giants" a little more than a few centimeters (1 inch) across. Their shells come in a wide variety of shapes—some look like overlapping flower petals, others like bulbous seed pods.

As the protists died or shed their armor, the tiny plates gently drifted down to the bottom of the sea. There they built up in layers, over thousands, then tens of thousands, then millions of years. The chalky shells formed a thick white sludge on the bottom of the sea that gradually thickened from inches to tens of feet. Millions of years later that sludge would become the White Cliffs of Dover in England as well as the chalk that writes on countless classroom blackboards around the planet.

A piece of chalk, under a microscope, may reveal the fossilized forams that long ago created it. The dust from that chalk, under a powerful electron microscope, may reveal the even tinier coccoliths that once sank slowly through a Cretaceous sea.

Although both kinds of protists produce chalk shells, they are very different from each other. Foram shells are dotted with tiny holes (the name comes from a Latin word meaning "opening") through which the protists send out pseudopods to gather food. Forams eat lots of other protists, and they themselves serve as food for other, larger creatures.

The coccoliths, on the other hand, come from protists that are a kind of algae. Scientists did not know this until about twenty-five years ago, although they had known about the beautiful shells for long before that.

Mammoths Among The Mummies

Fossilized foram shells make up a large part of the seafloor, and of the limestone that came from vanished sea bottoms. One famous fossil foram is known as *Nummulites,* the "coin stone," because it is large and round like a coin. Certain species within that genus can grow quite large by protist standards. Modern nummulites can reach an enormous 2 millimeters (.08 inch) across.

But 50 million years ago, nummulites grew much larger. Specimens 10 centimeters (4 inches) across can be easily seen in the limestone slabs used to build the Egyptian pyramids. And a species called *Nummulites millecaput* grew to an absolutely mind-boggling 160 millimeters (6.2 inches)—a single-celled protist giant! Even more astounding is that it lived for more than a hundred years. Today's nummulites can live for a year or two, at best.

Studies of *N. millecaput*'s fossils have shown that this foram grew extraordinarily slowly, increasing very gradually in size as it aged. And it grew in a sea unusually rich in nutrients.

At about four-fifths of an inch across, these fossil nummulites, or "coin stones," are extremely large cells; but some nummulites once grew eight times as large.

They just did not know what produced them. As it turned out, the shells are made by a group of free-swimming algae, called haptomonads, that have two distinct phases to their life cycle. In the first, they are "naked" swimming cells—that is, cells without shells—with two tails and a thread-like anchor that they use to attach themselves to rocks. The second phase is the "resting" phase, during which they cover themselves with the armored plates. Why they do that is not clear. But the plates may function like venetian blinds, controlling the amount of light the protist is exposed to.

DIATOMS

There is yet another large group of protoctists with shells, just as remarkable as the chalk-makers and perhaps even more beautiful. These are the radiolarians and the diatoms, single-celled protists with shells made not from calcium but from silica.

Silica is a combination of oxygen and the element silicon, and it is an extremely common and useful substance. We see it every day in the form of glass and sand. More rarely we see it in the form of opals and rubies. The shells that protists create from silica are stunningly sculptured. The shells of radiolarians often look like medieval helmets and weapons, adorned with slender spikes. Many diatom shells, on the other hand, look like exquisite, round pill boxes, perforated with rows of tiny holes. Others look like decorated peanuts, still others like stacked checkers. So small and fine are the details of these shells that they are used to test the accuracy of microscope lenses.

Diatoms are plentiful in the ocean today, and are represented by some 10,000 species. Diatoms may, in fact, be the second-most abundant form of life on the planet, outnumbered only by bacteria. There are many extinct diatoms also, perhaps as many as 100,000 species. Fossil diatoms, packed thickly on the floor of a long-ago sea, today form mineral beds a thousand feet thick. "Diatomaceous earth," a very slightly gritty substance made up

Magnified, a round diatom shows off its elaborate shell design. Diatom shells are always in two halves and are made of silica, as are sand, glass, and rubies.

mostly of ancient diatom shells, is an ingredient in products ranging from paint to toothpaste.

Some diatoms are loners, while others live stacked atop one another in long, stringy colonies. Still others live within the bodies of larger forams. But all the world's diatoms can be divided into two basic groups: "centric" diatoms, which are round; and "pennate" diatoms, which are shaped like needles or boats. Both kinds are photosynthesizers, like plants, and so they are grouped among the algae. But they have two different lifestyles. The round diatoms are floaters in the sea. With thousands of other microscopic bacteria and protoctists, and small animals, they make up the vast drifting menagerie of organisms known as plankton.

Pennate, or boat-shaped, diatoms also have a two-part glassy shell. In all, diatoms make up an enormous variety of life-forms, with some 10,000 species among them.

The pennate diatoms, though, are less passive. They rarely float near the ocean's surface. They are more at home on the sea bottom or attached to rocks along the shore. Not content to just drift through life, these diatoms push their way through the world in an odd and interesting manner.

Like their round cousins, the boat-shaped diatoms are made of two symmetrical half shells, or "valves." Between the valves is a narrow slit (technically, it is called a raphe) that runs the length of the diatom's body. To move, the diatom extends a thin, sticky strand through the slit at one end of its body. The strand sticks to whatever surface the diatom is on, and then, exposed to seawater, it hardens and becomes something like a pole. Inside the diatom, the other end of the pole is attached to a special outer layer of the cytoplasm. That layer now begins flowing toward the back end of the cell, dragging the embedded pole-end with it. Since the opposite end of the pole is attached to a rock or sand grain, the entire boatlike body of the diatom is pushed forward, and the pole is dragged through the slit toward the back end of the diatom. The process is much like a gondolier poling a gondola through a shallow Venetian canal. As the diatom goes by, the attached pole is broken off, and a new sticky strand appears at the front end for the next great push.

The diatom's sticky-strand method of movement is effective, even if it is not especially speedy. The fastest a diatom can move is 25 micrometers (about .001 inch) per second, which really is not too bad if the diatom is a typical 50 micrometers (.002 inch) or so from end to end. On a human scale, that speed is equivalent to a slow walk. It would be a very odd walk, however—kind of a *step,* pause . . . *step,* pause . . . *step,* pause . . . And it would be as much back and forth as forward. Diatoms may be determined, but they are not well directed.

Diatom Shell Game

Diatoms have a very fair system for dividing the family fortune among offspring. When a diatom reproduces—by splitting itself into two—each of the two cells gets one half of the parent's gorgeous two-part shell. Each new diatom then grows a new, slightly smaller half-shell that fits inside the "lip" of the old one.

The only problem with this process is that it means that each new diatom must be a little smaller than its parent. Any family that keeps this up long enough will soon find itself reproducing to the edge of nothingness.

The diatom solution? Sex, of a sort. Once the diatom has reproduced itself down to a minimum size—about two-thirds of its original girth—it produces a rebellious "child." This new diatom doesn't clothe itself in a shell like so many of its ancestors did. Instead it swims around naked until it bumps into another shell-less cell like itself. Then the two cells fuse. Once joined, the two cells are as big as the original diatom, and they— or rather, it—can grow a shell and start a new family line.

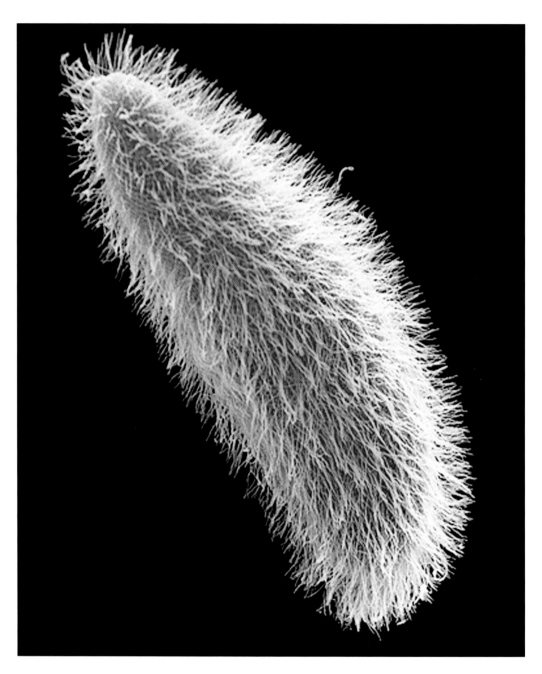

A paramecium is covered with tiny hairs, or cilia, that beat together like oars to propel the protist. (Color has been added to the image to make the cilia more visible.)

CHAPTER FIVE

Protist Paddlers

CILIATES

Protists equipped with undulopodia—cell tails—are able to move faster than slow-poling diatoms. By whipping its tail back and forth, a protist like *Euglena* can motor through the water at about a tenth of a millimeter, or 100 micrometers (.004 inch) per second. This is four times faster than the most ambitious diatom.

But even these speedsters are no match for the protists known as ciliates. Ciliates make up a large class of roughly 10,000 single-celled protoctist species, and they live virtually everywhere—in lakes, rivers, ponds, and rivers the world over. Their most distinguishing characteristic is the rows of small hairlike cilia (from the Latin word for "eyelash") that cover their entire body. These cilia are in fact shorter versions of the undulopodia of other protists, but they work a bit differently. Rather than whipping about frantically, the cilia all move together like well-coordinated oars to propel the protist swiftly through the water.

THE PARAMECIUM'S PROGRESS

Among the best known of the ciliates are paramecia. Biology students commonly catch a glimpse of paramecia through a microscope, zipping across their field of view. These slipper-shaped protists are often a student's first encounter with the dynamics of very small beings, and they offer a thrill as great as that felt by Leeuwenhoek when he first spied his animalcules more than three centuries ago. With their gracefully beating cilia, paramecia are quite animated and fun to watch. Like simple robotic toys, they move forward until they bump into something. Unless that something is food, they immediately reverse their oars and go in the opposite direction.

In truth, not even the most sophisticated toy can compare with a ciliate. It is easy to say, and to imagine, that the cilia are like tiny oars. But they are really far more complex. Think about what happens when we row a boat. We pull back on the oars, which in turn push against the water and propel us forward. At the end of our stroke, we lift the blades of the oars out of the water. As we do so, the boat continues gliding forward, and we get the oars into position to pull again. Assuming that we have been exercising regularly and that our muscles are in good shape, our only requirements are a boat that floats and a pair of strong, stiff oars.

A paddling paramecium may be working the same pond we are. But it faces an entirely different set of challenges. The first difference is that the paramecium cannot glide as our boat can. It is so small and so nearly weightless that it has no momentum, no force to keep it moving once its oars have stopped rowing. The water stops it dead. To a creature the size of a single cell, water is not the thin, fluid substance it is to a big human. To a protist, water is a thick, dense syrup. A paramecium swimming through a pond is equivalent to a human swimming through a pool of molasses.

The second difference is that for the paramecium there is no "out of the water." It cannot ever lift its tiny ciliate oars clear of the water, and so they are immersed all the time. The result is that any backward stroke will offset any forward stroke, and the paramecium will never move at all.

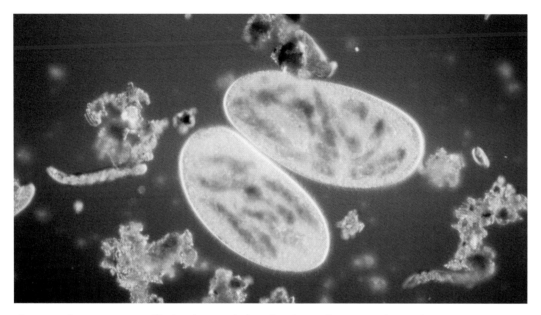

This pair of paramecia are filled with a meal of euglenids, smaller protists that, without cilia, are not nearly so speedy.

Obviously, the only way a paramecium can manage is by finding a way to push hard on the first stroke and hardly at all on the return stroke. And that is precisely how the cilia work. These marvelous bits of engineering somehow stay stiff on the forward stroke but then immediately relax and bend on the return. In their limp mode, they pass through the water with little resistance and so do not push the protist backward.

This mechanism works so well that cilia are employed for many different purposes by many different cells in many different organisms. For example, just as cilia can move a mobile creature through a liquid, so they can move a liquid past a stationary creature. This is exactly what cilia do in the cells that line the gills of a clam—as they wave back and forth they move the water over the gills.

Cilia do the same thing in the cells that line our own lungs and windpipe. They keep a thin mucous layer in motion to trap any stray unwanted particles we breathe in with our air.

Leishmania are parasites, living off of other organisms. In humans, these protists can literally eat away flesh or destroy the white blood cells of the immune system.

Troublemakers and Killers

Nearly all the hundreds of thousands of protoctist species on Earth pass beneath our notice and our knowledge—a natural consequence of their being invisible. But there are a handful of protoctists that we are very uncomfortably aware of, and about whom we have learned a lot. These are the few that, directly or indirectly, threaten our food supply, our health, and sometimes our lives.

Some of the most common troublemakers belong to the group known as the dinoflagellates, or the dinomastigotes. As with many protist/protoctist names, scientists disagree on which is proper. The "flagellates" part of *dinoflagellates* refers to two whipping tails that are characteristic of these species. Scientists who wish to emphasize that protists have undulopodia, and not true flagella, prefer *dinomastigotes* instead (*mastigote* refers to tiny hairs growing from the undulopodia).

More interesting is the *dino* part of the name. Because some of these protists cause such great trouble for humans, it is tempting to suppose that *dino* is the same "terrible" tag that we pin on the dinosaurs. In fact, the dinosaur's *dino* comes from *deino,* (which means "terrible") while the dinomastigotes' name comes from *dino*, which means "rotating" or "whirling." It refers to the way these protists swim: one tail stretches out behind the protist, while the other goes sideways, across its body. With both tails whipping, the protist whirls.

THE RED MENACE

There are perhaps 20,000 species of these whirling protists, all of which live in the sea, and most of which are little known. Many, though, make their presence known to sailors at night. Like fireflies, they produce an internal light, and they can cast an eerie glow upon the surface of the sea. A few dinoflagellates, however, are famous for a different skill. These are the choreographers of the events known as red tides.

A "red tide" such as this one in Australia is caused by a sudden, large increase in the population of poison-producing protists that can kill sea animals and sicken people.

The term is misleading. Red tides are sometimes but not always red, and the events are not tied to any tide. What they are, in the calm words of objective scientists, are "harmful algal blooms"—which means that they are sudden and dramatic increases in a dangerous protist population. The greatly increased numbers of protists release a toxin, or natural poison, that can kill fish and shellfish, and sicken the people who eat them.

Why they sometimes behave this way is not clear. But the behavior clearly works. Dinoflagellates have been around for nearly 600 million years.

FISH KILLER: *PFIESTERIA*

Protists rarely make front page headlines. But a few years ago one, named *Pfiesteria piscida,* became very big news. It was engaged in mass murder off the coast of North Carolina. In the summer of 1997 *Pfiesteria* populations "bloomed" across Chesapeake Bay, and thousands of fish started turning up dead. Then reports of illness among swimmers and fishermen began coming in. Authorities quickly declared large areas of the bay and several rivers leading into it off-limits to humans.

Pfiesteria had been identified only a decade earlier, though it had surely been around for eons. Its discoverer was biologist JoAnne Burkholder, and she has spent many years now investigating *Pfiesteria*'s behavior. She has found that *Pfiesteria,* like many dinoflagellates, has a complex life cycle. It has at least twenty-four distinct stages. In some of them it is a whirling swimmer. In others it becomes more like an amoeba, crawling along the bottom of the sea or on the skin of animals. During most of its stages it feeds on other protists or bacteria or on tiny bits of fish tissue floating in the sea.

Pfiesteria is a natural inhabitant of the sea. So long as there are not too many of these protists, and so long as they are quietly hunting microscopic prey, they are not a problem for us. Every once in a while, though, something happens that makes *Pfiesteria* change its habits. Scientists do not yet know what triggers the change, but it may be a chemical signal given off by a school of fish swimming through the water. When *Pfiesteria* get a whiff of the signal, they transform themselves from silent lone stalkers to an army bearing chemical weaponry.

The energized *Pfiesteria* release a toxin that stuns the fish and prevents them from moving. The poison then acts on the fishes' skin, causing sores to form. The fish start bleeding. Bits of skin begin to flake off. The *Pfiesteria* launch an all-out attack, and the fish become a meal for millions of microscopic munchers.

The power of the protist toxin is astounding. These single-cell creatures can kill animals as large as a blue crab or a large-mouth bass. And as Dr. Burkholder discovered, just breathing in their poison can make a human quite ill. While working on *Pfiesteria* in her lab, several of her colleagues became nauseous, had trouble breathing, and became confused. Some experienced a loss of memory.

Red-tide dinoflagellates like *Pfiesteria* can be dangerous, but they are only occasional threats. Far more problematic, and far more important historically, are a group of protists that have evolved to live as parasites. They are dependent on the bodies of other living creatures for their survival. Several have found very comfortable homes in the bodies of humans.

FLESH EATER: *LEISHMANIA*

A dozen different species make up the group of protists that go under the genus name *Leishmania*. Like all protist parasites, *Leishmania* leads a complicated life, and it changes its form repeatedly. It normally travels from one human to another by hitching a ride on a biting sand fly. When a sand fly bites into a person's skin, the protist parasite enters the victim's bloodstream. Once there it worms its way into the best possible hiding spot: the white blood cells that are normally responsible for killing such alien invaders. Over time *Leishmania* has evolved ways to keep our defense

The bloodsucking sand fly is more than a pest—it is a carrier of *Leishmania* protists, which can enter a human bloodstream when the fly starts to dine.

system from finding it in its hideout, and so it is left free to go about its business. Unfortunately for us, its business is eating and reproducing. The side effects of that activity can be devastating.

Each species of *Leishmania* causes a different disease in humans. One may cause only a painful blister on the skin. Another, though, may literally eat away the flesh of a person's face. Yet another may destroy a person's immune system, the defense army of white blood cells, leaving him vulnerable to death from the slightest infection.

EVIL AUGER: *TRYPANOSOMA*

Horrible as *Leishmania* parasites are, they do not come close to being the worst protists for humans. They are easily beat by *Trypanosoma*.

Trypanosomes are long, thin, flat protists related to the one-tailed euglenids. But while euglenids swim in freshwater ponds and saltwater bays, trypanosomes have evolved to swim in the watery tissues of our bodies. Their swimming style gives them their name. *Trypanon,* is Greek for "auger" or "corkscrew," and it vividly describes how they swim through our bloodstream.

Trypanosomes have earned a place in the human parasite hall of fame because they cause African sleeping sickness. Despite its mild-sounding name, sleeping sickness is a killer. As the trypanosomes progress through a person's body, they gradually destroy different organs, leaving their victim weaker and weaker. Eventually they attack the brain, and kill their human host.

With luck (from the parasites' point of view) before their human home is demolished they will be given a ride to a new residence. Their transportation is the biting tsetse fly. Tsetse flies and their trypanosome stowaways have played an enormous role in shaping the history of Africa. The flies range over much of the continent below the Sahara, and they have caused the deaths of millions upon millions of people. In addition, because one form of sleeping sickness affects cattle and another affects horses, for thousands of years people were unable to raise these animals in many parts of Africa. The threat to humans and livestock effectively prevented, or at least slowed, the building of cities and industries in much of sub-Saharan Africa. In many ways, the fate of an entire continent was determined by a single-celled protoctist.

Modern medicines and modern methods of controlling fly populations have helped, but the trypanosomes remain a problem. Tsetse flies still keep more than 4 million square miles of otherwise prime African pastureland free of cattle. And sleeping sickness continues to weaken and kill hundreds

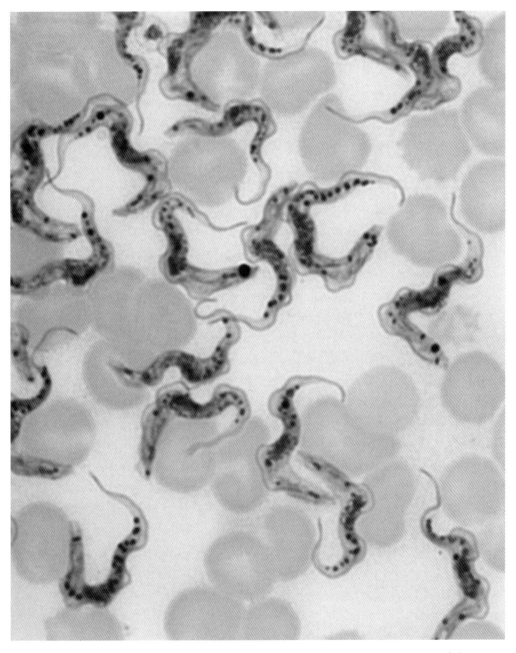

Corkscrewing trypanosomes can destroy a series of human organs. They are the cause of sleeping sickness, which kills hundreds of thousands of people yearly.

of thousands of Africans every year, particularly in countries disrupted by war or too poor to afford proper medicines.

Sleeping sickness is a giant of a killer. But it is dwarfed by another protist-caused disease: malaria. Like other parasitic diseases, malaria today is mainly a disease of the tropics. But its range in the past has been vast. It was a plague in ancient Rome, and it has ravaged Europe, Asia, and every other continent except Antarctica. In the United States it haunted not only the Deep South but also the mid-Atlantic states. In the nineteenth century it made its way as far north as New York City and North Dakota.

Malaria has been able to succeed so well because it flies in the body of a very versatile insect, the mosquito—and because the creature that causes the disease is a very clever protist named *Plasmodium.*

How clever is *Plasmodium?* A single-celled *Plasmodium* may have no brain, but it is still clever enough to take advantage of both its human and mosquito host. The protist mates and matures in the mosquito. When it is ready to move on, it releases a substance that makes the mosquito especially hungry. The mosquito responds by biting as many humans as possible. When the insect sinks its needle-nosed proboscis (the mouthparts used for piercing and sucking) into human skin, *Plasmodium* escapes into the victim's bloodstream. Once inside it quickly swims to the liver, where it begins making thousands of copies of itself. Eventually the white blood cells detect the invaders. But by the time the white blood cells get to the liver to begin their counter-attack, the protists have moved into the red blood cells, which they proceed to destroy. Before they are done, some of these infected cells will likely be sucked up by the next passing mosquito and carried to another human.

Malaria has been so widespread and so deadly that some researchers calculate that it has killed half the people who have ever lived. Today, even

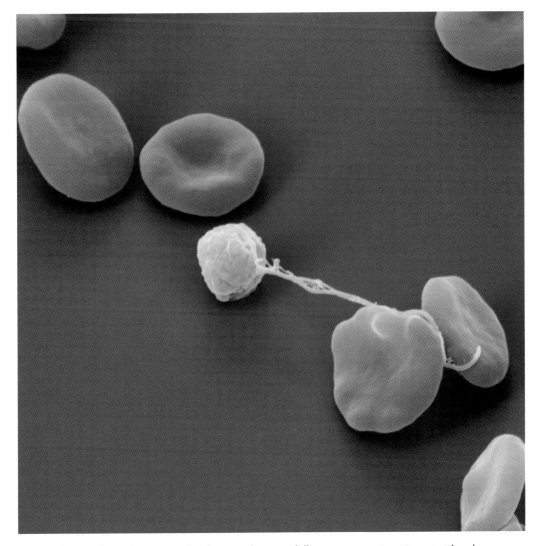

Plasmodium (yellow), the cause of malaria, is the great killer among protists. Once inside a human bloodstream, it invades and destroys oxygen-carrying blood cells (red).

with our best medicines, it continues to kill more than 2.5 million people every year. Most of those victims are young children. Malaria severely weakens many millions more people, and leaves them vulnerable to a long list of other diseases.

In Africa, *Plasmodium* has not only shaped the destiny of a continent but also the genes of its people. The parasite kills because it invades a victim's red blood cells, the cells that carry oxygen from the lungs to all parts of the body. Naturally, during the thousands of years that people have been battling *Plasmodium,* the human body has tried out all sorts of defenses. Any defenses that have been successful have been passed from parents to children, in their genes. In Africa, one of those successful defenses against malaria, strangely enough, is a deformed red blood cell that can cause another killer disease: sickle-cell anemia.

When we are conceived, we each receive two genes that determine the shape of our red blood cells—one gene from our father, the other from our mother. People who inherit two normal genes produce round blood cells that flow smoothly through the body's arteries. People who inherit two sickle-cell genes, however, produce red blood cells that are sickle, or crescent, shaped. These cells tend to get stuck in the blood vessels, especially in the capillaries, the thinnest vessels. The usual result is that parts of the body do not get as much oxygen as they need, and the person suffers an early and painful death.

As it turns out, though, people who inherit just one sickle-cell gene and one normal gene make enough normal red blood cells to function. At the same time, they get some protection against malaria—the deformed, sickle-shaped cells prove to be unusable homes for the *Plasmodium* parasite.

Evolution has presented Africans with a tough bargain. Mathematically, the lives saved by the protection against malaria apparently balance out those lost to sickle-cell anemia. But that is little consolation to the families of those afflicted with the genetic disease. Worse, the legacy of the fight against *Plasmodium* lives on even when the protist has ceased being a threat. People descended from Africans might have the sickle-cell gene even though their ancestors left Africa long ago. Today, in the United States, 10 percent of African Americans still carry one copy of the double-edged gene, protecting them against a protist they are unlikely to meet.

The Protist That Starved a Nation

A one-celled protist can have an effect on humans grossly out of proportion to its size. Take the case of *Phytophthora infestans*.

P. infestans causes a disease called potato late blight. Within days after the parasite takes up residence in a potato plant, it turns the leaves and stem into a purplish-black slime, and the tuber—the potato itself—into worthless pulp. It moves rapidly, and it can destroy a whole field in less than a week.

In the 1840s *P. infestans* demolished the potato fields of Ireland, wiping out the crop that so many families depended on for food. In the horrible famine that followed, 1.5 million people—one-fifth the population—starved to death. Another million fled their homeland, many for the United States.

The Irish men, women, and children who made it to America settled mostly in the large cities of the Northeast, far removed from any farmlands. Boston, Philadelphia, and New York were completely remade by the flood of Irish immigrants, and the changes can be seen to this day. Ireland too still feels the effects of losing so many of its people. Two nations, across the width of a great ocean, were transformed by the might of a protist.

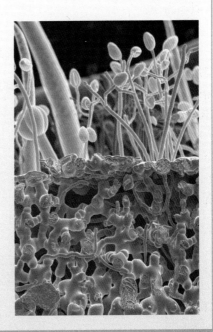

The gray stalks of *Phytophthora infestans* push through the surface of a potato plant leaf—this protist alone led to the starvation of millions in Ireland in the 1840s.

Single-celled algae make up most of the vast carpet of sea life called plankton, and all animal life ultimately depends on these protists for both food and oxygen.

The Importance of Protoctists

Given the horrendous suffering these few protists cause, and the invisibility of most of the others, many people might think the world would be quite fine without the whole Kingdom Protoctista. But they would be very mistaken.

The uncountable trillions of protoctists on Earth are immeasurably important, even for us humans. First of all they are invaluable as food. Their worth goes way beyond the absolute necessity of certain choice seaweeds for delicious sushi. It even goes beyond the critical importance of algae for properly thickened ice cream, or even as a source of vitamins and minerals and medicines. The protoctists' true value lies not in their use as food for us but as food for others.

The largest algae, such as the kelp, provide food and shelter for all kinds of sea life, from abalone to urchins. These seaweed eaters then become food for larger animals, such as otters and fish, who become food for such larger meat eaters as sharks, and seals—and humans too.

CRITICAL FLOATERS

But the most important algae are not the giant multicelled hundred-footers or even their shrimpy one-foot cousins. By far, the most important algae are the microscopic one-celled protists who live in the warm sunlit surface of the seas, where they float along with the immense drifting army of tiny organisms we call plankton.

Plankton is a general term we use for any life-forms that float atop the ocean. Traditionally grouped among the plankton are both "animal" forms, or zooplankton, and "plant" forms, or phytoplankton. Many plankters (the word for individual floaters) are indeed animals. Jellyfish are among them, along with the shrimplike "krill" that, by the ton, fill the bellies of hungry whales. But many, many, many more plankters are protists. Among them are the microscopic photosynthesizers from which Earth's entire web of life is woven.

Phytoplankton are the leaves and grass of the sea. Just as all animal life on land ultimately depends on plant life for its existence, all life in the sea depends on photosynthesizing plankton. They feed the other protists and sea animals just as surely as the grass feeds the antelope that feeds the lion. They are the base of a great food web.

But they are more than that. They are also the base of the great cycle of oxygen production. We all learn as children that we need plants on Earth to supply the oxygen we need to breathe. But few of us realize that a huge number of the "plants" we rely on are in fact protists. Single-celled algae may produce 50 percent of the world's oxygen. Without them we would all suffocate.

At the same time that they fill the air with oxygen, they, like plants, remove carbon by taking in the carbon dioxide that we and all other animals exhale. But we humans are adding much more carbon than this to the air. This extra carbon comes in the form of gases pouring from the tailpipes of our cars and the smokestacks of our factories. So far, the plants and the algae have been up to the task. But there is only so much carbon we humans can comfortably handle in the air we breathe. If something were suddenly to threaten the health of the carbon-vacuuming algae, our health would be threatened also.

Unfortunately there are several things affecting the health of the algae. And they all are tied to one broad human activity: pollution.

BIG THREATS TO LITTLE BEINGS

The first problem comes from those carbon gases we are adding to the air. Because they tend to trap heat, like a blanket, they are helping to cause global warming, a gradual increase in temperatures around the world. Like plants, algae are sensitive to changes in temperature, and in the amount of sunlight and nutrients they get. They too have seasons when they "bloom" and reproduce and seasons in which they are quiet. The other protists and animals who feed on the algae rely on this cycle. They are all part of an extremely complicated system. Any change in any part of the system—say, a warming of certain parts of the ocean, or a melting of polar ice—can cause unexpected changes elsewhere.

The second problem is the "ozone hole" over Antarctica—not a hole, actually, but a thinning of a layer of the atmosphere, caused by certain chemicals we humans used to release into the air. This layer normally blocks out harmful ultraviolet radiation—the part of sunlight that causes sunburn. We have stopped using the chemicals, but the hole will take several more decades to heal. In the meantime, more radiation than normal comes in through the hole.

Sitting under the hole is the Southern Ocean, an algae-rich part of the sea. The extra radiation can harm these algae, just as it can harm the surface layer of skin cells on a human arm. Many large sea animals, from penguins to seals to whales, feed in the Southern Ocean. And of course they feed on an ever-decreasing line of smaller animals and protists that ultimately feed on algae. How any change in the algae population might ultimately affect them is not known.

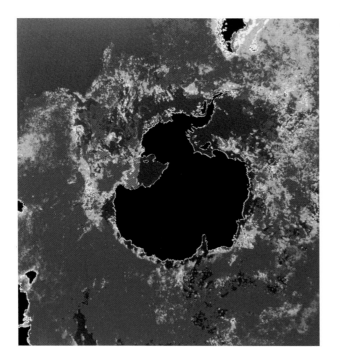

Colors show summer algae growth around Antarctica (central black). Red areas have the most algae; yellow, the second most; then green, then blue. Anything interfering with that growth could threaten animals from krill to squid to fish, birds, seals, and whales.

Finally there is the problem caused by direct pollution of the oceans, and of the rivers and streams that flow into them. Some of this pollution comes from chemicals dumped carelessly by factories. Other pollution comes from the millions of tons of chemical fertilizers washed off farmlands by rain. Still other pollution comes from human sewage. Whether delivered by pipelines or waterways, all of it eventually ends up in the sea.

The effects of this unnatural addition to the ocean are unpredictable. Some pollutants act as poisons, of course, and simply kill whatever life they contact. But the real problems come from the opposite effects. Fertilizers and sewage act as food for the protists. They don't kill them—they allow them to thrive. Sometimes they cause such an explosion of algae growth that all other life gets choked off. This seems to be what is happening now in the Gulf of Mexico, where it is fed by the mighty, and chemical-laden, Mississippi.

Sometimes the chemical stew feeds a protist that humans would rather see starved. Many scientists think that human sewage funneled into Chesapeake Bay is what led to the sudden increase in fish-killing *Pfiesteria* in recent years.

In large laboratory vats, scientists grow plankton that have been collected from the sea to study how environmental changes might affect the health of our planet.

SURVIVAL INSTINCTS

We would be wise to pay more attention to the protists. We would not be here were it not for these humble ancestors of ours. The reverse—that the protists would not be here were it not for us—is not even close to true. If all humans everywhere were to disappear tomorrow, nearly all members of the protoctist kingdom would go on living happily, completely unaware that for a brief moment in Earth's history we humans existed. The protists that have evolved to be parasites in humans might have a hard time, of course. But some of them would adjust. Protists are a tough bunch. They know how to wait out hard times.

Sixty-five million years ago, when something—probably an asteroid—slammed into Earth, life suffered one of its great extinctions. All the land-dwelling dinosaurs died, and the magnificent winged pterosaurs dropped

These dinoflagellates, called *Ceratium hirundinella,* could help save us from ourselves— they reveal the effects of pollution in freshwater lakes and streams.

from the skies. All the great seagoing "monsters" of old—the ichthyosaurs and the mosasaurs and the plesiosaurs—sank out of sight, never to rise again.

The water-dwelling protists were hard hit also. More than half of all plankton species vanished. Nearly three-quarters of the chalk-armored coccolithophorids died, along with a whopping 92 percent of chalky forams. They all settled down in the sediments to a future as, well, chalk.

But the diatoms were barely affected. Less than a quarter of their kind went the way of the dinosaurs. The rest produced cysts, went into their resting states, and waited for better times to come. When it was time again for their moment in the sun, they awoke, and thrived.

They are thriving still. We, their brainy ever-so-distant relatives, should strive to thrive with them.

algae—Protoctists that get their energy through photosynthesis; among the algae are both single-cell protists and giant seaweeds.

asexual reproduction—The creation of a new organism without sex, meaning without the addition of genes from another cell; bacteria and some protists reproduce asexually, by splitting in half.

bacteria—Members of the kingdom Monera; simple cells without a nucleus.

binomial nomenclature—The system in which each type of living thing is assigned two names: a broad genus name and a more "specific" species name.

chlorophyll—A green-colored substance that permits cells to turn sunlight into energy.

chloroplasts—Chlorophyll-containing units in plant and protoctist cells.

chromosomes—Thin strands in the nucleus of eukaryotic cells that carry the genes.

cilia—Short cell "whips" or "tails" that move back and forth rapidly; they can propel a cell through a fluid, or move fluid past a cell.

cyst—A hardened resting stage of a protist, often formed when conditions for reproduction are poor.

cytoplasm—The fluid interior of a cell.

DNA—The chemical that makes up the genes of an organism; the DNA is a cell's instruction manual, telling it how to grow and what to do.

eukaryote—A cell with a nucleus; all life-forms except bacteria are made of eukaryotic cells.

flagellum—The "tail" of a bacterium, which twirls or corkscrews rather than whips back and forth.

gene—A bit of information, in the form of DNA, that makes up a specific instruction for an organism, such as what shape of red blood cell to produce; genes are passed from parents to offspring.

genus—A category of classification that is one level higher than species; plural is genera

host—An organism that serves as the home of a parasite; both humans and mosquitoes, for example, serve as the host for the parasite that causes malaria.

malaria—A disease caused by the protists known as plasmodia; malaria has killed more people over the course of history than any other disease.

membrane—A thin, flexible lining that surrounds a cell or an organelle.

microbe—Any living thing too small to be seen without a microscope.

microtubule—A very thin tube found in eukaryotic cells; microtubules are used for the movement of cytoplasm inside the cell, and in undulopodia outside the cell.

mitochondria (singular: mitochondrion)—The "power plants" of animal and many protoctist cells; these specialized units make use of oxygen to produce energy.

nucleus (plural: nuclei)—The "kernel" in a eukaryotic cell that contains the DNA; bacteria do not have nuclei.

organelle—Any smaller unit within a cell, such as a chloroplast or mitochondrion.

organism—An individual living thing; organisms can be single-celled, like a protist, or multicelled, like a human.

photosynthesis—The process by which plants and many protoctists make energy by harnessing sunlight.

plankton (singular: plankter)—The huge collection of small and microscopic animals, protoctists, and bacteria that float on or near the surface of the sea; plankton are the base of the ocean's food web.

plastid—Any of the units that carry on photosynthesis in a cell; chloroplasts are green plastids, while rhodoplasts are red plastids.

prokaryote—A cell without a nucleus; all bacteria are prokaryotic cells.

protist—A microscopic or single-celled protoctist.

protozoa—An early name for what were thought to be microscopic animals; these "first animals" are what we now properly call protists.

pseudopod—A "false foot," or a pushed-out extension of the cell, used by amoeba-like protists for crawling around and engulfing food.

rhodoplast—A red-colored energy-producing organelle inside red algae.

sexual reproduction—The making of a new organism through the combination of genes from other, separate organisms.

species—The basic unit of classification that defines a "specific" type of animal or plant; all humans, for example, are one species, but there are many cat species, including house cats and cougars.

symbiosis—The act of two organisms coming to live together as one.

taxon—Any of the units of classification for living things; species is one taxon, genus is another.

taxonomy—The science of classification.

undulopod (plural: undulopodia)—The "whips" of eukaryotic cells; unlike the flagella of bacteria, undulopodia whip back and forth, are longer, and are made of microtubules bundled together.

vacuole—A chamber inside the cell of a protist such as an amoeba, in which food is sealed.

xanthoplast—A yellow-colored energy-producing organelle inside yellow and yellow-green algae.

PROTOCTIST PHYLA

The protoctist kingdom contains a huge number of species—anywhere from 250,000 to 600,000. How all those individual species are best grouped into genera, then families, then classes, orders, and finally phyla is a matter of great disagreement among scientists. They even disagree as to how many phyla the kingdom should have: some say twenty, others propose as many as fifty. One widely accepted grouping, shown here, names thirty phyla. But as scientists learn more about protoctists and their mysterious ways, that number may change.

A phylum is the largest, most inclusive category after kingdom. At the level of phylum, house cats, for example (phylum Chordata), are grouped together not only with all other mammals but with all reptiles, birds, and fish as well, along with any other animals that have a spinal chord. To find an animal in a different phylum, we need to look at something with a completely different body design, for example, an insect (phylum Arthropoda).

Pictured here are representatives of just four protoctist phyla. They are related, but they are as distant from one another as a giraffe is from a jellyfish, a starfish from a sponge, or an earthworm from a clam.

Saprolegnia

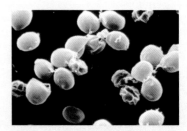

Cryptosporidium parvum

Giardia

Sargassum filipendula

Saprolegnia is commonly known as water mold because it appears as a fungus-like infection of fish. Of course, it is not a member of the fungus kingdom at all. It is a protist, belonging to the phylum Oomycota.

Giardia and *Cryptosporidium* might seem to be closely related because they can both cause serious intestinal diseases in humans. But their similar effect on people does not actually reflect any close relationship between them. *Giardia* belongs to the phylum Archaeprotista, a group containing some of the most ancient members of the kingdom. They have rather simple cell structures, with no energy-producing mitochondria. *Cryptosporidium* is in the phylum Apicomplexa, which is made up of much more complex protists, nearly all of which are parasites that take on different forms during the various stages of their life cycle.

Finally, *Sargassum,* a form of brown algae, belongs to the phylum Phaeophyta, which means "brown plants." Like green, red, and yellow algae—cousins so distant they all have phyla of their own—brown algae were once thought to be members of the plant kingdom. Some scientists still prefer to think of them that way. But most are now content to see them as fascinating members of the wondrous kingdom of protoctists.

KINGDOM PROTOCTISTA
(30 different phyla*)

Archaeprotista	Cryptomonada	Hyphochytriomycota
Microspora	Discomitochondria	Haplospora
Rhizopoda	Chrysomonada	Paramyxa
Granuloreticulosa	Xanthophyta	Myxospora
Xenophyophora	Eustigmatophyta	Rhodophyta
Myxomycota	Diatoms	Gamophyta
Dinomastigota	Phaeophyta	Actinopoda
Ciliophora	Labyrinthulata	Chlorophyta
Apicomplexa	Plasmodiophora	Chytridiomycota
Haptomonada	Oomycota	Zoomastigota

*Source: *Five Kingdoms: An Illustrated Guide to the Phyla of Life on Earth* by Lynn Margulis and Karlene V. Schwartz.

F U R T H E R   R E A D I N G

Hoagland, Mahlon, et al. *Intimate Strangers: Unseen Life on Earth* (companion book to PBS documentary). Washington, D.C.: American Society of Microbiology, 2000.

Maton, Anthea. *Parade of Life: Monerans, Protists, Fungi, and Plants.* Englewood Cliffs, NJ: Prentice Hall, 1994.

Rainis, Kenneth G. and Bruce J. Russell. *A Guide to Microlife.* Danbury, CT: Franklin Watts, 1996.

Silverstein, Alvin and Virginia Siverstein. *Monerans & Protists.* Brookfield, CT: Twenty-First Century Books, 1996.

Snedden, Robert. *A World of Microorganisms.* Chicaco, IL: Heinemann Library, 2000.

WEB SITES

Hunting Micro-aliens: The First Voyage
http://www.microscopy-uk.org.uk/mag/artfeb01/micalien1.html

Introduction to the Eukaryota: Fungi, Protists, Plants, Animals...
http://www.ucmp.berkeley.edu/alllife/eukaryota.html

Micrographia—Protozoa: An introduction to protozoa/protoctista
http://www.micrographia.com/specbiol/protis/homamoeb/
amoe0000.htm

National Geographic's Virtual Tour of Monterrey Bay
http://www.nationalgeographic.com/monterey/ax/primary_fs.html

Smithsonian Magazine: The Sargasso Sea
http://www.smithsonianmag.si.edu/smithsonian/issues98/
nov98/sargasso.html

Stalking the Mysterious Microbe! — Protists
http://www.microbe.org/microbes/protists1.asp

University of Wisconsin Protist Images
http://botit.botany.wisc.edu:16080/images/130/Protista_I

What are Microbes? Algae, Protozoa, Slime Molds, and Water Molds
http://www.microbeworld.org/htm/aboutmicro/microbes/
types/protista.htm

BIBLIOGRAPHY

The author found these books especially helpful when researching this volume.

Asimov, Isaac. *Asimov's Biographical Encyclopedia of Science and Technology,* 2nd rev. ed. Garden City, NY: Doubleday & Company, 1982.

Breger, Dee. *Journeys in Microspace: The Art of the Scanning Electron Microscope.* New York: Columbia University Press, 1995.

Desowitz, Robert S. *Who Gave Pinta to the Santa Maria? Torrid Diseases in a Temperate World.* New York: W. W. Norton & Company, 1997.

Fortey, Richard. *Life: A Natural History of the First Four Billion Years of Life on Earth.* New York: Alfred A. Knopf, 1998.

Franklin, Harold M. *The Way of the Cell: Molecules, Organisms, and the Order of Life.* New York: Oxford University Press, 2001.

Gould, Stephen Jay. *Eight Little Piggies.* New York: W. W. Norton & Company, 1993.

—-. *Ever Since Darwin.* London: Burnett Books Ltd., 1978.

—-.*The Panda's Thumb.* New York: W. W. Norton & Company, 1980.

—-. *Wonderful Life: The Burgess Shale and the Nature of History.* New York: W. W. Norton & Company, 1989.

Gould, Stephen Jay, ed., *The Book of Life: An Illustrated History of the Evolution of Life on Earth.* New York: W. W. Norton & Company, 1993.

Kunzig, Robert. *The Restless Sea: Exploring the World Beneath the Waves.* New York: W. W. Norton & Company, 1999.

Margulis, Lynn. *Symbiotic Planet: A New View of Evolution.* New York: Basic Books, 1998.

Margulis, Lynn and Dorion Sagan. *Microcosmos: Four Billion Years of Microbial Evolution.* Berkeley, CA: University of California Press, 1997.

Margulis, Lynn and Karlene V. Schwartz. *Five Kingdoms: An Illustrated Guide to the Phyla of Life on Earth*, 3rd ed. New York: W. H. Freeman and Company, 1998.

Margulis, Lynn, Karlene V. Schwartz, and Michael Dolan. *Diversity of Life: The Illustrated Guide to the Five Kingdoms*, 2nd ed. Sudbury, MA: Jones and Bartlett Publishers, 1999.

McGowan, Chris. *Diatoms to Dinosaurs: The Size and Scale of Living Things.* Washington, D.C.: Island Press, 1994.

McMahon, Thomas A. and John Tyler Bonner. *On Size and Life.* New York: Scientific American Library, distributed by W.H. Freeman and Company, 1983.

"Nature Insight: Malaria," *Nature* 415, no. 6872, 7 February, 2002.

Sagan, Dorion and Lynn Margulis. *Garden of Microbial Delights: A Practical Guide to the Subvisible World.* Cambridge, MA: Harcourt Brace Jovanovich, 1988.

Thomas, Lewis. *The Lives of a Cell.* New York: Viking, 1974.

Wills, Christopher. *Yellow Fever, Black Goddess: The Coevolution of People and Plagues.* Reading, MA: Addison-Wesley, 1996.

Zimmer, Carl. *Parasite Rex: Inside the Bizarre World of Nature's Most Dangerous Creatures.* New York: The Free Press, 2000.

I N D E X

Page numbers in **boldface** are illustrations and charts.

Marc Zabludoff, former editor in chief of *Discover* magazine, has been involved in communicating science to the public for more than two decades. He has written two other books in this series for Marshall Cavendish, on reptiles and on insects. His books for the AnimalWays series include *Spiders* and future works on beetles and monkeys. Zabludoff lives in New York City with his wife and daughter.